Usborne

100
Christmas
things to make and do

Contents

3

Fingerprinted robins

1. Dip a fingertip into brown paint and print it onto a piece of paper. Then, do several more prints.

2. For the robins' tummies, dip your finger into some red paint and print it onto each brown shape.

3. Wash your hands. Then, dip your little finger into some white paint and print a spot on each red tummy.

4. Dip the edge of a piece of cardboard into some brown paint and print two lines for the tail, like this.

5. When the paint is completely dry, draw a beak and eyes on the robins with a black felt-tip pen.

6. Draw two wings and legs with the black pen. Add three small lines at the end of each leg for the feet.

Christmas stockings

1. Paint lots of stripes with different paints, across a piece of white paper. Do some thick ones and some thinner ones.

2. When the paint is dry, use felt-tip pens to draw spots, stripes and other patterns on some of the thicker lines.

3. Draw a stocking on the paper and cut it out. Draw around it on plain paper. Cut out shapes for the top, heel and toe, and glue them on.

Mosaic snowflakes

1. Cut small rectangles of thick white paper. Paint each one with a different shade of blue ink or paint. Then, leave them to dry.

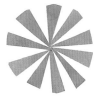

2. Cut ten long, thin triangles from one of the painted papers. Glue them in a circle on a piece of white paper.

3. Cut little triangles from a different piece of painted paper and glue them around the circle. Then, cut five small rectangles.

4. Glue the rectangles in the gaps between some of the little triangles. Then, glue three thin triangles between each of the rectangles.

5. Cut small triangles and glue them in star shapes at the ends of the thin triangles. Make the points touch each middle triangle.

6. To finish the mosaic snowflake, cut long, thin triangles and glue them at the end of each of the small rectangles.

Angel paperchain

Make the small circle touch the bottom of the big one.

1. Fold a piece of white paper in half, with the short edges together. Then, fold it again.

2. Draw a circle that almost touches the top of the paper. Draw a smaller circle inside.

3. Draw a long triangle for a dress. Add two little feet at the bottom of the dress.

4. Draw big sleeves almost touching the edges of the paper. Add hands that reach the edge.

5. Using scissors, cut around the angel, but don't cut along the folds on the hands.

6. Open out the chain of angels. Draw their faces and hair. Make each one look different.

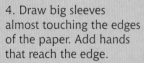

7. Draw patterns on their dresses and halos. You could glue glitter on them, too.

8. Decorate the other side of the chain. Draw the back of their hair and wings.

9. Make more chains. Join them together by pressing a piece of tape onto the angels' hands.

Snowman card

1. Cut a rectangle from thick blue paper. Then, cut a piece of thick white paper exactly the same size. Fold both of them in half.

2. Unfold the blue paper. Draw a wavy line across one half of the card for snow. Draw the outline of a snowman above the line.

You don't need this piece.

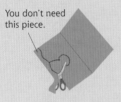

3. Use a pair of scissors to cut along the line for the snow, then around the snowman and along the line for snow again.

4. Spread glue on the top half of the blue card. Then, press one side of the white card onto it. Make sure that the edges line up.

5. Spread glue on the other half of the blue card, around the snowman shape. Then, close the card, pressing it down onto the white card.

6. Draw eyes and a mouth with a black felt-tip pen. Cut shapes from paper for the hat, nose and buttons, then glue them on.

Busy elves

1. Use a pencil to draw an oval for a head. Press very lightly as you draw. Add a pointed ear and two little lines for the neck.

2. Draw a teardrop-shaped body. Add arms, then draw legs with tiny feet. Add a pointed hat, a frill around the neck and a skirt, too.

3. Either mix water with red paint and fill in the body, arms and hat, or fill them in with felt-tip pens. Fill in the skirt, legs and frill in green.

4. Then, fill in the face and hands with watery paint or a felt-tip pen. Draw a circle on top of the hat and add some hair. Fill them in, too.

5. When the paint is dry, paint or draw rosy cheeks. Draw a present on the elf's hand and add ribbons and a big bow.

6. Use a thin brown felt-tip pen to draw over all the pencil lines. Add lines in her hair and looping lines on her skirt. Draw a belt, too.

15

Snowball truffles

To make about 15 truffles, you will need:

- 175g / 6oz / 1 cup white chocolate chips
- 25g / 1oz / 2 tablespoons unsalted butter
- 50g / 2oz plain sponge cake or 15 vanilla wafers
- 4 tablespoons shredded or desiccated coconut
- small paper cases

Keep stirring until everything has melted.

1. Fill a large pan a quarter full of water and heat it until the water bubbles. Then, remove the pan from the heat.

2. Put the chocolate chips and butter into a heatproof bowl. Wearing oven gloves, carefully put the bowl into the pan.

3. After two minutes, stir the chocolate and butter until they melt. Wearing oven gloves, carefully lift the bowl out of the water.

4. Crumble the cake or wafers into fine crumbs. Add the crumbs to the chocolate mixture and stir everything well with a wooden spoon.

5. Spread the coconut on a plate. Scoop up some of the chocolate mixture with a teaspoon and put it into the coconut.

6. Roll the mixture in the coconut to make a ball, then put it in a paper case. Make more truffles, then put them in the refrigerator for one hour.

Pretty boxes

1. Rip some tissue paper into pieces. Brush the pieces with household glue and press them all over a box and its lid.

2. Brush glue all over the top and the sides of the lid. Then, sprinkle glitter all over the lid and leave it to dry.

3. When the glue is dry, glue sequins around the edge of the lid. Then, glue sequins in the middle too. Leave the glue to dry.

Winter painting

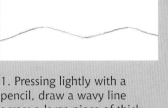

1. Pressing lightly with a pencil, draw a wavy line across a large piece of thick white paper. This will be the top of the snow.

2. Using a thick brush, fill in the sky above the wavy line with dark blue or purple watery paint. Then, leave the paint to dry.

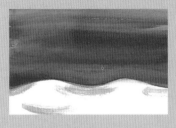

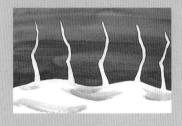

3. For the shadows on the snow, dip a dry brush into watery blue paint. Then, brush a few wavy lines across the paper.

4. When the paint is dry, use thick white paint to paint several tree trunks on the sky. Make the trunks twist a little, like this.

5. Paint some branches coming out from the trunks. Then, use the tip of a thin paintbrush to add lots of small twigs.

6. Use the tip of the brush to add lots of little dots between the trees, for snowflakes. Then, paint a crescent moon in the sky.

Crown Christmas card

Use a dry brush so that you leave brushmarks.

1. For textured papers for the crowns, paint scraps of paper or cardboard. Brush on another shade when the paint is dry.

2. For a pointy crown, cut a rectangle from a piece of textured paper. Cut two deep triangles into the top edge.

3. Cut a thick strip of red wrapping paper, shiny paper or textured paper and glue it across the bottom of the crown.

Glue the gold strips vertically.

4. Cut a strip of gold paper and glue it across the points. Then, trim the strip at each end and between the points.

5. Cut thin strips of gold paper and glue them on the red paper. Then, glue an orange textured strip across the bottom.

6. For a rounded crown, draw a shape like this on one of the pieces of textured paper or shiny paper. Then, cut it out.

7. Glue a strip of paper across the bottom and glue little strips along it. Then, cut three thin triangles and glue them on.

8. Cut a round shape from paper and glue it on the top of the crown. Then, fingerprint a jewel in the middle.

9. Make more crowns from the papers. Then, glue them onto a folded piece of cardboard or thick paper, to make a card.

Sparkly angels

Use a sparkly pipe cleaner if you have one.

Fold the paper, short ends together.

1. Cut a pipe cleaner in half. Then, for the angel's head, push a bead about a quarter of the way along one of the pipe cleaners.

2. Bend the top of the pipe cleaner around to make a halo above the head. Push the end of it into the hole in the bead.

3. For the dress, cut a strip of crêpe paper or tissue paper about 30cm (12in.) long and 6cm (2½ in.) wide. Fold it in half.

4. Gather the paper along the top edge and wrap it tightly around the pipe cleaner, just below the head. Hold it in place.

5. Wind some thin thread around the top of the paper several times. Then, tie the two ends tightly to secure the thread.

6. For the wings, cut two pieces of sticky tape and dip the sticky sides into some glitter. Then, trim off the ends, like this.

Use more than one pin if you need to.

7. Lay the wings, glittery-side down. Then, fold in the corners at the flat end of each one to make a pointed shape.

8. Overlap the pointed shapes on the back of the angel. Secure the wings by carefully pushing pins down into the dress.

9. Curl the end of the pipe cleaner just below the bottom of the dress. Tie some thread through the halo, for hanging.

25

Snowflake ornaments

1. Draw around a mug twice on a piece of white paper, then draw around it twice on red paper. Cut out the circles.

2. Cut a strip of thick cardboard about the width of one of the circles. Cut two shorter, narrower strips, too.

3. Pour some red and white paint onto an old plate. Dip the edge of the longest piece of cardboard into the white paint.

4. Press the edge onto one of the red circles. Print two more lines in an 'X', dipping the cardboard into the paint each time.

5. Use the other pieces of cardboard to print shorter lines on the snowflake. Then, print a snowflake on the other red circle.

Use other edges of the cardboard for the red paint.

6. Print red snowflakes in the same way on the white circles, then leave them until the paint is completely dry.

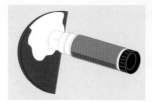

7. Fold each circle in half, along one of the long printed lines. Then, spread glue on one half of one of the red circles.

8. Press one half of a white circle onto the glue, matching the edge and the fold. Then, spread glue on its other half.

9. Press on the other red circle, matching the edge and fold as before. Then, make a loop in a piece of thread and tape it inside.

10. Glue one half of one of the red circles and press on the remaining white circle. Then, glue the last two halves together.

Penguins on the ice

Some paint will seep into the creases.

1. Draw all over a piece of white paper with a white wax crayon or a white candle. Then, scrunch the paper into a tight ball.

2. Flatten the paper and paint it all over with blue paint. Then, rinse the paper under cold running water, rubbing it gently.

3. Leave the paper to dry. Then, draw a line for the horizon and another line for the sea. Fill the sky and sea with blue paints.

4. Paint another line along the edge of the sea. Draw some curved lines for blocks on the ice and paint them, too.

Use thick paint.

5. Draw a body, then add a line inside it for the white part on the penguin. Add wings, a beak and feet.

6. Paint the black parts and let them dry. Then, fill in the white parts. Finally fill in the beak and feet.

29

Tree top fairy

 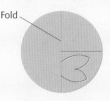 

1. Lay a plate on some paper and draw around it. Cut out the circle. Then, fold the circle in half and open it out.

2. Using a pencil, draw a line from the middle of the circle to its edge. Then, draw a wing below the line, touching the fold.

3. Cut up along the fold, around the wing, along the fold again and along the line. Then, cut halfway down the wing, like this.

4. Bend the wing over and gently hold it down, like this. Then, carefully draw around the edge of the wing with a pencil.

5. Open out the paper shape and cut around the second wing. Then, cut halfway down into the wing, like this.

6. Bend the body around so that the cuts in the wings are touching. Slot them together, then curve the body with your hands.

7. Cut out a head and hair, and glue them together. Cut out arms and glue hands onto them. Glue everything onto the body.

8. Cut out legs and shoes. Draw stripes on the legs, then glue the legs onto the shoes. Then, tape the legs inside the body.

9. Cut out a crown and a wand from shiny paper and glue them on. Then, decorate the fairy with stickers and sequins.

Tracing paper star card

1. Use a thick gold pen to draw a squiggly line all over a piece of tracing paper. Then, draw another line with a thin pen.

2. Draw a star on the tracing paper and cut it out. Then, draw a similar star on gold paper and cut it out, too.

3. Put some glue on the back of the tracing paper star and press it onto the gold one, so that the points overlap, like this.

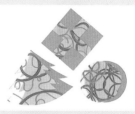

4. Use the same method to make more shapes, such as ornaments, packages and Christmas trees.

5. For a simple card, glue the shape onto a piece of thick, folded paper. Draw an outline with glitter glue.

6. To make a more elaborate card, glue the shape onto a piece of paper. Then, glue the paper onto a folded card.

Printed reindeer

1. Glue a piece of thin cardboard onto a sponge cloth. Draw a body and head on the cardboard.

2. Cut out the shapes. Spread thick red paint on an old plate. Dip the body shape into the paint.

3. Press the sponge onto a piece of paper. Then, print the head shape next to the body.

Twist the cardboard.

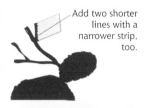

Add two shorter lines with a narrower strip, too.

4. Cut a strip of cardboard for the legs. Dip the edge into the paint, then print four legs.

5. Dip the cardboard into the paint again and print two lines on the reindeer's head for antlers.

6. Print lots more short lines on the antlers and three lines for the tail. Then, print the ears.

You could draw spirals on the spots.

7. Spread light blue paint on the plate. Fingerprint spots on the body and one on the nose.

8. When the paint is dry, outline the reindeer with a black pen. Add eyes, a mouth and hoofs.

Bouncing snowman

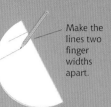

Make the lines two finger widths apart.

1. Draw around a large plate on white paper. Cut out the circle and fold it in half.

2. Draw a line from the fold almost to the edge. Draw one from the edge almost to the fold.

3. Draw another line from the fold. Make it two finger widths again below the second line.

4. Draw lines all the way down. Then, cut along them. Keep the paper folded as you cut.

5. Unfold the circle and flatten it. Draw around a saucer for a head. Cut it out and glue it on.

6. Cut a hat and nose from paper and glue them on. Then, draw eyes and a mouth.

7. Cut out arms and boots from paper and glue them to the back of the body.

8. Tape a piece of ribbon to the back of the head. Then, gently stretch the body down.

9. Press a piece of poster tack onto the bottom of the body, to help the snowman bounce.

Festive trees

1. Place a mug or a cup near one end of a long rectangle of dark paper. Draw around the mug with a pencil, pressing lightly.

2. Draw a trunk and a plant pot below the circle. Then, draw a large bow with flowing ends, a little way down the trunk.

3. Use a light blue pencil to draw a small holly leaf in the middle of the circle. Then, draw more holly leaves around it and fill them in.

4. Continue drawing little holly leaves at different angles until you reach the edge of the circle that you drew in step 1.

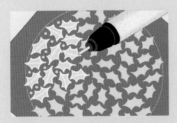

5. Draw around each leaf with a silver or gold felt-tip pen and add some little dots for berries in the spaces between some of the leaves.

6. Outline the trunk, the bow and the plant pot with a gold or silver pen. Then, carefully erase the pencil circle when the ink is dry.

Christmas collage

  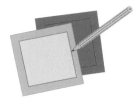

1. Draw a line down the middle of some thick red paper. Add two lines across it to make six squares.

2. Lay a corner on green paper, lining up the edges and pencil lines. Draw around the corner.

3. Cut out the square, then draw around it on two other pieces of green paper.

4. Cut out the green squares and glue them onto the red paper. Trim the edges if you need to.

5. Decorate each square with a different Christmas picture. Cut them from paper or fabric.

6. To make the bird's tail, fold a piece of paper into a zigzag. Glue it at one end.

 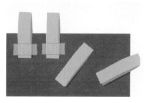 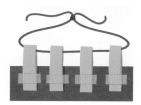

7. Add details to each picture with glitter, glitter glue and sequins, or glue on shiny paper.

8. Fold four strips of green paper in half, then tape them to the back of the collage, at the top.

9. To hang the collage, push a long piece of thread through the loops and knot the ends.

Spotted paper

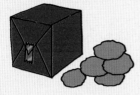 

1. Wrap your present. Then, rip lots of circles from a different piece of wrapping paper.

2. Glue the circles all over the wrapped present. Make the circles bend over the edges of the present.

3. Rip lots of smaller circles from different wrapping paper. Then, glue them onto the bigger circles.

Springy gift tags

1. Cut a star from thin cardboard. Decorate it with felt-tip pens, stickers or glitter.

2. Wind a pipe cleaner tightly around a pencil or felt-tip pen. Then, slide it off gently.

3. Push the last two coils of the pipe cleaner together at one end. Glue it to the back of the star.

Tissue paper present

4. Do the same to the coils at the other end. Put some glue on it and press it on your present.

1. Cut a large square from a double layer of tissue paper. Lay your present in the middle.

2. Gather the paper up around the present, then tie it tightly with a piece of gift ribbon.

Polar bear pop-up card

The pieces of paper should be the same size.

Keep the paper folded as you cut.

Nose cut

1. Fold a piece of white or cream paper in half. Do the same with a piece of blue paper.

2. On the white or cream paper, draw half of a bear's head against the fold, like this.

3. Cut around the head. Make a cut for a nose. Cut out shapes along the edge for fur, too.

4. Lift the nose and fold it flat onto the front, like this. Crease the fold. Fold it behind, too.

5. Open out the head. Push a finger through the nose from the back, so that it stands up.

6. Use felt-tip pens to draw a mouth and eyes. Carefully fill in the nose.

Match the middle folds.

7. Put glue on the back of the head, but not on the nose. Press the head onto the blue paper.

8. Cut a rectangle of wrapping paper for a present. Glue it on below the head.

9. Cut two paws from white paper. Glue them on. Add claws with a black felt-tip pen.

1. Cut a piece of bright cardboard or thick paper the same size as this book, when it's opened out.

2. For the tree, fold a large rectangle of green paper in half, with the long sides together.

3. Draw a diagonal line and cut along it. Then, cut small triangles from the open edge.

—Fold —Fold

You will need 24 altogether.

Glue here.

4. Cut a white shape for the snow. Glue it on. Open out the tree and glue it in the middle.

5. To make the doors, draw circles, squares and other shapes. You need 24 doors altogether.

6. Cut out the shapes. Spread glue along one edge of each shape and press it on.

Make sure your picture is smaller than the door.

7. Draw a different Christmas picture behind each door. Make them smaller than the doors.

8. Cut lots of Christmassy shapes from bright paper. Then, glue them onto the calendar.

9. Use a black felt-tip pen to write a number on each door. Number them from 1-24.

Snow cloud meringues

To make about 30 meringues,
you will need:

* 2 eggs, at room temperature
* 100g / 4oz / ½ cup granulated sugar
* sugar sprinkles

Heat your oven to 110°C, 225°F,
gas mark ¼, before you start.

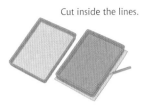

Cut inside the lines.

1. Draw around a baking sheet on baking parchment. Cut out the shape and put it in the tray. Then, do the same with another tray.

2. Break one egg on the edge of a large bowl. Then, pour it carefully onto a saucer, so that the egg yolk doesn't break.

3. Hold a cup over the yolk and carefully tip the saucer over the bowl so that the egg white dribbles into it.

4. Repeat steps 2-3 with the other egg so that both egg whites are in the bowl. You don't need the egg yolks.

5. Whisk the egg whites with a whisk until they are really thick. They should form stiff points when you lift the whisk up.

6. Add a tablespoon of sugar to the egg white and whisk it in well. Whisk in the rest of the sugar a tablespoon at a time.

7. Scoop up a teaspoon of the meringue mixture. Use another teaspoon to push it off onto one of the baking trays.

8. Make more meringues until you have used all the mixture. Then, sprinkle a few sugar sprinkles over each one.

9. Bake them for 40 minutes, then turn off the oven. After 15 minutes, remove the trays and leave the meringues to cool.

Fairy lantern decorations

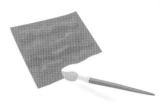

1. Mix some household glue with water, so that it is runny. Then, brush the glue all over one side of a piece of paper.

2. Sprinkle silver glitter over the wet glue, then leave the glue to dry. When it is dry, turn the paper over.

3. Mix some pink paint with a little water. Then, paint all over the piece of paper and leave the paint to dry completely.

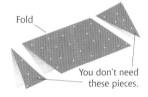

Fold

You don't need these pieces.

4. When the paint is dry, draw little dots all over it with glitter glue. Then, draw a pencil line down the middle of the paper.

5. Draw three lines across the paper, to make eight rectangles the same size. Then, cut along all the lines you have drawn.

6. Fold one of the rectangles in half, along its length. With the fold at the top, cut a triangle off each end.

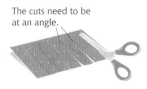

Tape this end, too.

7. Cut lots of slits along the folded edge of the paper, but don't cut as far as the unfolded side. Then, open out the paper shape.

8. Put a drop of glue at the top and bottom of one end of the shape. Bend the shape around until the ends meet. Press them together.

9. Tape a piece of thread inside the lantern, as a handle for hanging. Then, make more lanterns from the other rectangles.

Santa picture

1. Spread red and pink paint on some kitchen paper towels, on a newspaper.

2. Cut the end off a big potato and throw it away. Cut the rest of the potato in half.

3. Dip one half of the potato into the red paint. Press it onto the middle of a piece of paper.

4. Cut a small potato in half, then dip one half into pink paint and print Santa's face.

5. Dip your finger into the red paint and finger paint a hat. Then, paint the arms, too.

6. Dip your finger again and print his legs and mittens. Then, leave the paint to dry.

7. Fingerprint a white beard on his chin. Keep dipping your finger and printing blobs.

8. Fingerprint more white blobs on the edge of his hat, body, arms and legs.

9. Using a black felt-tip pen, draw Santa's face. Draw his boots and fill them in.

Christmas reindeer

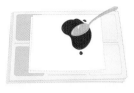

1. Cut a potato in half, lengthways. Then, turn it over and cut away two pieces at the sides, to make a handle.

2. Lay a few kitchen paper towels in a pile on a newspaper. Pour brown paint on top and spread it out with an old spoon.

3. Holding the handle, press the flat side of the potato firmly onto the patch of brown paint, then lift it up.

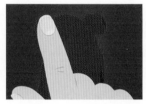

4. Press the potato onto some paper to print the reindeer's head. Press the potato into the paint again and do more prints.

5. For the reindeer's ears, dip your finger into the brown paint. Fingerprint an ear on either side of the head.

6. When the brown paint is dry, pour red paint onto the paper towels and spread it out. Dip your finger into the paint.

7. Fingerprint a red nose near the bottom of each head. Then, use a black felt-tip pen to draw two eyes on each one.

8. When the paint is dry, draw two long lines for antlers. Then, draw a few smaller lines on each side of the long lines.

55

Christmas crown

Draw it
a little way
from the bottom.

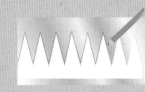

The crease marks
the middle.

1. Cut a rectangle of thick
paper that fits around your
head. Then, cut a little off
one end.

2. Fold the rectangle with
its short ends together.
Fold it twice more, then
draw a line across it.

3. Fold the paper in
half with its long sides
together. Then, press it to
make a crease at one end.

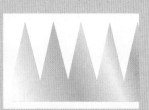

Crease

Cut
halfway
down.

4. Draw from the crease
to each end of the
horizontal line. Then, cut
along the slanting lines.

5. Unfold the paper
and lay it on some thin
cardboard. Draw around
the shape and cut it out.

6. Cut a triangle off one
end, leaving a strip at
the bottom. Then, cut
down into the strip.

Use your fingers.

7. At the other end, cut
up into the last triangle.
Make the cut the same
length as the first one.

8. Slot the cuts at each
end together, with the
ends inside. Then, secure
them with tape.

9. Bend each point out,
like this. Then, decorate
the crown with beads,
sequins and glitter glue.

Santa face collage

1. Tear an oval of brown or pink paper from an old magazine for the face. Then, glue it onto a piece of paper, like this.

2. Tear lots of pieces of white and cream paper from a magazine. It doesn't matter if they have patterns or lettering on them.

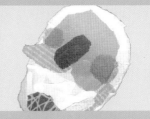

3. Rip small pieces from the paper and glue them around the face for the hair. Add ripped pieces for his beard and whiskers, too.

4. Tear two small circles of pink paper or tissue paper for the cheeks and an oval one for the nose. Then, glue them onto the face.

5. Cut or tear a hat shape from red patterned paper and glue it on. Then, rip a white or cream circle and glue it onto the tip, too.

6. Add eyes with white paint or correction fluid. Leave them to dry, then use a pencil to draw a mouth, and pupils in the eyes.

Snow scene cartoon

Erase the lines where the trees overlap the hill.

1. Draw a wavy line for the hills, across a piece of white paper. Then, draw trees along the line.

2. Draw a circle for a girl's head. Add her body, arms and hands. Then, draw her legs and feet.

3. Draw a hat and some hair. Draw her eyes, nose and mouth. Then, add a line for a scarf, too.

4. Draw a sled with a curve along the front edge. Add lines joining it to her hand.

5. Decorate the girl's clothes. Then, draw a seat and some footrests on the sled.

6. Fill in the girl and sled with felt-tip pens. Then, outline them with a thin black pen.

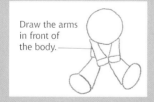

Draw the arms in front of the body.

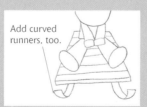

Add curved runners, too.

7. For someone on a sled, draw the head and arms. Then, add the body, legs and feet.

8. Draw a rectangle for the sled around the body. Draw lines across it, and a front edge.

9. Draw a hat, ears and flowing hair. Add eyes, a nose and a mouth, then fill her in with pens.

Shepherd collage

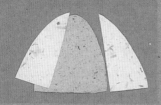

1. For a shepherd's body, cut a curved shape from brown paper. Glue it onto a large piece of paper, then glue on two shapes for the cloak.

2. Cut out a headdress from white paper. Glue on a face, a beard and a red headband. Then, glue the headdress onto the body.

3. Cut strips of paper and glue them onto the cloak. Then, cut out a shepherd's crook and glue it on. Add a paper hand on top.

4. Cut a large oval shape from paper for a sheep's body. Then, cut a small oval for a head and glue it on. Glue on eyes and ears, too.

5. Cut out strips of paper for the legs and tail and glue them on. Cut another little strip and a triangle shape for the collar and the bell.

63

Fingerprinted snowmen

Dip your thumb back into the paint every few prints.

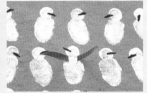

1. Dip your thumb into some white paint and print several rows of thumbprints across a piece of dark paper.

2. Dip the tip of your first finger into the white paint and print a snowman's head on each of the thumbprints.

3. Cut a thin strip of thick cardboard. Dip the end into red paint and print a nose on each head. Print them at different angles.

4. When the paint is dry, get an adult to cut two small slits on either side of some of the snowmen, just below their head.

5. Push a narrow piece of gift ribbon down through one slit, then up through the other slit, from the back of the paper.

6. Tie the ends of the ribbon together to make a scarf around the snowman's neck. Trim the ends if they're too long.

Keep the top of the cardboard in one place.

7. For a pointy hat, dip the end of another thin strip of thick cardboard into some paint, then twist it above the head.

8. When all the paint is dry, draw stick arms and fingers on each snowman. Draw them in different poses. Add eyes, too.

9. Add buttons to some of the bodies. Then, draw different mouths, making them laugh, shout, look upset, surprised or asleep.

Folded star ornaments

1. Cut several strips from thick paper, making them the same width. Then, paint all the strips with the same paint.

2. Glue the strips of paper together to make one really long strip which is at least three times the width of this single page.

3. Start by folding one end of the strip over, like this. Crease the fold well. The fold will form one edge of the star.

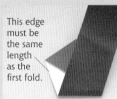 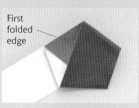 

This edge must be the same length as the first fold.

First folded edge

4. Now, fold the long end of the strip upwards, so that the left-hand edge is exactly the same length as the first folded edge.

5. Then, fold the paper behind, making sure that it runs along the first folded edge. All the edges should be the same length.

6. Keep folding the long strip around the five-sided shape, making sure that all the edges and folds match neatly.

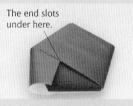  

The end slots under here.

Don't be afraid to press the edges hard.

Be careful as you push the needle through.

7. When you reach the end of the long strip, push the loose end under the strip as far as it will go and crease its fold.

8. Press in each side of the shape firmly to make into a rough star shape. Then, pinch each point in turn to make them neat.

9. Decorate the star. Then, ask an adult to push a needle and thread through one point and tie the ends to make a loop.

Sparkly hearts

Fold ——

1. Fold a piece of thin cardboard in half. Draw half a heart on it, then cut out the shape.

2. Lay the heart on thick paper. Draw around it four times. Then, cut out all the hearts.

3. Fold each heart in half, then open them out. Paint one side of a heart with white glue.

4. Sprinkle glitter over the glue and leave it to dry. Do the same to the other three hearts.

5. When the glue is dry, fold the hearts with the glitter inside. Brush glue on the top of one.

6. Press one half of another heart onto the glue, lining up the edges. Wait for the glue to stick.

7. Glue on another heart in the same way. Make a loop in a piece of thread and tape it inside.

8. Spread glue on both halves of the last heart and press it on, over the end of the thread.

You could make more decorations, using these shapes.

Printed gift tags

Decoration

1. Dip the edge of a piece of cardboard into gold or orange paint. Print a criss-cross pattern on thin cardboard.

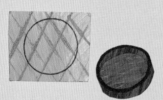

2. When the paint is dry, lay a small lid onto the piece of cardboard and draw around it. Then, cut out the circle.

3. Use felt-tip pens to decorate the circle with stripes and zigzags. Tape a piece of ribbon to the back.

Snowman

You don't need this piece.

1. Ask an adult to cut the ends off a carrot with a knife, making a big end and a small end.

This will be the body.

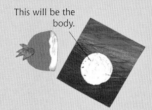

2. Dip the big end of the carrot into thick white paint. Press it onto a piece of thin cardboard.

3. Print a head with the small end of the carrot. When it's dry, draw a face, hat and buttons.

71

Zigzag card

Middle fold

1. Cut a long, thin rectangle of thick paper or very thin cardboard. Fold it in half lengthways and crease the fold well.

2. Fold the top layer over until it meets the middle fold. Turn the card over and fold it in the same way, to make a zigzag.

3. Open the card and draw a wavy line from one side of the card to the other, like this. Use a pencil and press lightly.

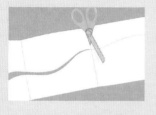

The shapes are shown in yellow here so you can see them.

4. Cut along the line you have drawn but stop at the last fold. Then, cut down the fold from the top, as far as the pencil line.

5. Fold the card into a zigzag again. Then, use a white wax crayon to draw some stars and a moon. Press hard as you draw.

6. Open the card, then paint over the stars and moon with blue paint as far as the pencil line. The shapes will resist the paint.

Overlap the little trees.

7. While the sky is drying, draw lots of dots on some thick paper with the white wax crayon. Then, paint green paint over the top.

8. When the paint is dry, cut out about eight little triangles for the trees. Make them slightly different sizes.

9. Arrange the trees on the different layers and glue them on, making sure not to glue the layers together.

Snowflake fairies

1. Lay a mug on a piece of white paper. Draw around it, then draw around it on some purple paper, too. Then, cut out the circles.

2. Fold the white circle in half, then fold it in half twice more. Cut out lots of triangles around the edges of the paper.

3. Brush household glue over the snowflake. Sprinkle it with glitter, then let it dry. Then, glue it onto the purple circle.

The fold needs to be on this side.

4. Cut the snowflake in half. For a skirt, cut one half into two pieces. Then, cut a shape for the body from the smaller piece.

5. Glue the skirt onto a piece of paper, then glue on the body. Cut out a purple sash and glue it on, where the pieces join.

6. For the wings, draw around the mug and cut out the circle. Fold it in half three times, then draw half a wing shape, like this.

Keep the paper folded.

7. Cut along the line you have drawn, then cut a few triangles along the fold, like this. Then, open out the wings.

8. Spread glue over the wings. Sprinkle them with glitter, then let the glue dry. Glue the wings next to the body, like this.

9. Cut out a head and some hair and glue them together. Cut out arms, legs and a crown and glue them all on. Then, draw a face.

Cheesy Christmas stars

To make about 25 stars, you will need:

- 150g / 6oz / 1¼ cups self-raising flour*
- half a teaspoon of salt
- 75g / 3oz / ¼ cup butter or margarine
- 75g / 3oz / ⅔ cup cheese, finely grated
- 1 egg and 1 tablespoon of milk,
  beaten together
- a star-shaped cutter
- a greased baking sheet

Heat the oven to 200°C / 400°F / gas mark 6, before you start.

*In the US, use self-rising flour.

1. Sift the flour and salt through a sieve. Add the butter or margarine and rub it with your fingers to make fine crumbs.

2. Leave a tablespoon of the grated cheese on a saucer. Add the rest of the cheese to the bowl and stir it in.

3. Put a tablespoon of the beaten egg and milk mixture into a cup. Mix the rest into the flour to make a dough.

Roll out the dough so it's slightly thinner than your little finger.

4. Sprinkle flour onto a clean work surface. Roll out the dough with a rolling pin, then use the cutter to cut out star shapes.

Use a pastry brush.

5. Cut out more stars. Brush the stars with the rest of the egg mixture, then sprinkle them with the rest of the cheese.

6. Put the stars onto the greased baking sheet. Bake them in the oven for eight to ten minutes, until they are golden.

Penguin giftwrap

1. Make a pile of kitchen paper towels, then place them on a thick layer of old newspapers.

2. Pour some thick black paint onto the paper towels. Spread it out with the back of a spoon.

3. Use a knife to cut a big potato in half. Then, cut away two sides, to make a handle.

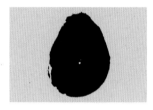

4. For a body, press the potato into the paint. Press it onto some paper, then print more bodies.

5. When the paint is dry, use a smaller potato to print a white tummy on each penguin.

6. Dip a brush into some orange paint. Paint a curved beak near the top of the penguins.

7. Dip a thin brush into black paint and paint two curved black flippers on each penguin.

8. For the penguins' feet, paint two orange triangles at the bottom of their bodies.

9. Paint a white eye on each penguin. Then, add a black dot when the white paint has dried.

Decorated angels

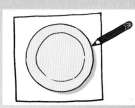

1. Put a small plate onto a piece of thick paper. Then, use a pencil to draw around it.

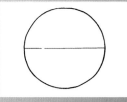

2. Cut out the circle you have drawn. Then, draw a faint line across the middle of the circle.

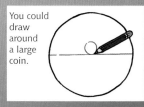

You could draw around a large coin.

3. For the head, draw a small circle in the middle of the big circle, just above the line, like this.

Cut along this line.

These will be the wings.

4. Draw a line around the circle. Then, draw a line from the edge to the head and cut along it.

5. Draw two curved lines, one on either side of the line across the middle. Cut out the shapes.

6. Draw four triangles around the edge, like this, then cut them out. These make the wings.

Arms

Head

Don't cut this part.

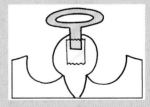
Decorate the angels' skirts with stars and spirals.

7. Cut around the arms and the head, shown here in red. Don't cut through the neck.

8. Erase any pencil lines you can see. Then, fold the wings and the arms forward. Crease them well.

9. Decorate the angel with felt-tip pens, or draw shapes with glue and sprinkle them with glitter.

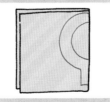

10. Turn the angel around and bend the ends around to make a cone. Tape the ends together.

11. To make a halo, fold a piece of paper in half. Draw the shape shown here and cut it out.

12. Open out the halo and flatten the fold. Tape the halo to the back of the angel's head.

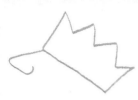  

1. Use a pencil to draw a crown at an angle near the top of a piece of paper. Then, add a nose.

2. Draw a beard below the nose with curved lines inside it. Then, add a headdress.

3. Draw a long shape for the body. Add a flowing cloak, then add pointed slippers, too.

Don't fill in the crown.

4. Draw sleeves and hands. Draw a circle for the gift, then erase any lines that overlap.

5. Fill in the face and hands with watery paint. Add red cheeks. Then, fill in the clothes, too.

6. When the paint is dry, draw over the outlines with a black pen. Add an eye and lines on the beard.

7. Use a gold pen to fill in the crown and decorate the headdress. Draw lines on the beard.

8. Decorate the sleeves and body with gold stripes and spots. Fill in the top of the gift, too.

9. Draw gold stripes and patterns on the cloak. Then, draw and paint two more wise men.

Robin decorations

1. Cut a strip of white paper about the height of this book. Bend it around to make an oval and glue it together, like this.

2. For the eye, cut a short strip of white paper. Roll it around a pencil and glue the end. Glue it inside the body.

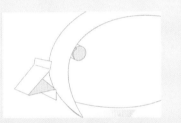

3. Cut a strip of paper for the beak. Fold it in half, then bend a little bit back at each end. Glue the ends onto the body.

4. Then, cut a strip of red paper. Bend it into a teardrop shape and glue the ends. Glue it inside for the bird's tummy.

5. Glue on a strip for a tail. Make two cuts in it, then curl the end around a pencil. Tape on some thread for hanging.

Angels with sparkly wings

Draw little circles on the cheeks with a red pastel, then smudge them.

1. Use a pink pencil to draw the outline of a head, neck and dress. Fill in the face, neck and shoulders with a chalk pastel. Then, draw hands and legs.

2. Use a black pencil to draw two curved lines for eyes and eyelashes. Add a smiling mouth. Then, draw little wings beside her shoulders.

3. Fill in the top of the dress and the sleeves with a yellow pastel. Then, fill in the rest in white and smudge the pastels together a little.

4. Add wavy lines with red and yellow pastels for frills on the dress. Draw a red and yellow halo above the head and add little red shoes.

5. Draw some hair with a red pastel and smudge it a little with your finger. Then, add some curly lines to the hair with an orange pastel.

6. Spread glue onto the wings and sprinkle them with glitter. Leave the glue to dry, then shake off any excess glitter.

Painted tissue giftwrap

1. Cut a piece of tissue paper about the size of this page, then fold it in half. Fold the paper in half again, two more times.

2. Dip a clean paintbrush in clear water and paint it all over the folded paper. Do this until the paper is really damp.

3. Paint a stripe of pink ink across the paper. Paint it again until the ink soaks all the way through the folded paper.

4. Paint a purple stripe across the top and bottom. Let the ink soak into the paper and mix with the pink ink.

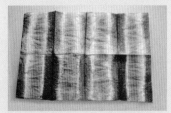

5. Keeping the paper folded, leave it until it's completely dry. Then, carefully unfold the paper and smooth it flat.

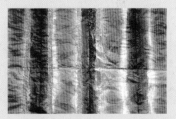

6. Brush stripes across the paper with glue. Sprinkle the glue with glitter and leave it to dry, then shake off any excess.

Stocking decorations

1. Fold a piece of bright, thick paper or thin cardboard in half, with the short sides together, like this.

2. Use a pencil to draw a stocking shape on the folded paper, with the fold on one side of the stocking.

3. Using a pair of scissors, cut out the stocking, making sure that you don't cut along the folded edge.

4. Open out the stocking and spread glue along one edge. Then, fold the stocking again.

5. Press down firmly on the stocking, making sure that the edges line up. Then, leave the glue to dry.

6. Decorate your stocking with glitter, stickers, pens or pencils. Add cut-out paper shapes and sequins, too.

Glittering snowflakes

1. Lay an old CD on a piece of thin white paper and draw around it with a pencil. Cut out the circle you have drawn.

2. Fold the paper circle in half, then fold it in half twice more. Cut lots of little triangles around the edges.

3. Gently unfold the paper to see your snowflake. Lay it on a flat surface and smooth it flat with your fingers.

4. Lay the CD on scrap paper and brush some glue around the middle of it. Sprinkle it with glitter and let it dry.

5. Shake any extra glitter off the CD. Put lots of little dots of glue on one side of the snowflake and press it on the CD.

6. Let the glue dry, then cut a long piece of thread and tape it to the back. You could then glue another snowflake on top.

Frost fudge

To make about 50 pieces of fudge, you will need:

- 350g / 12oz / 2 ²/₃ cups icing sugar*
- 75g / 3oz / 6 tablespoons unsalted butter
- 4 teaspoons milk
- ½ teaspoon vanilla essence
- 75g / 3oz / 2 cups pink and white marshmallows
- 2 tablespoons sugar sprinkles
- a shallow 18cm (7in.) square tin or pan

*Use powdered sugar in the US.

Put the bowl to one side until step 6.

1. Lay the tin or pan on a piece of greaseproof paper. Draw around it with a pencil, then cut out the square, just inside the line.

2. Use a paper towel to wipe cooking oil onto the sides and bottom. Press in the paper square and wipe it with oil.

3. Use a sieve to sift the icing sugar into a large bowl. Then, make a small hollow in the middle of the sugar with a spoon.

Use a pair of kitchen scissors.

4. Put the butter, milk and vanilla essence into a small pan. Then, cut the marshmallows in half and add them to the pan.

5. Gently heat the pan. Stir the mixture every now and then with a wooden spoon, until everything has melted.

6. Pour the mixture into the hollow in the middle of the sugar. Quickly stir everything together, until the mixture is smooth.

Press the sugar sprinkles into the fudge with your fingers.

Try not to knock off the sugar sprinkles.

7. Pour the fudge into the tin or pan. Sprinkle on the sugar sprinkles, then put it in a refrigerator for two hours.

8. Loosen the edges of the fudge with a blunt knife. Then, carefully turn it out onto a board and remove the greaseproof paper.

9. Turn the fudge over and cut it into small squares. Put the fudge in an airtight container, then chill it in the refrigerator for two hours.

Winter street scene

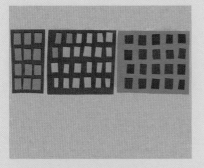

1. Cut out big squares for buildings and small squares for windows. Glue on the windows, then glue the buildings onto the top of a piece of paper.

2. Brush thick, white paint over the paper for snow. Use the tip of a brush to add lots of blobs of snow over the building and above them.

3. Cut out shapes for coats and jackets, and their sleeves, then glue them onto the background. Draw heads, and boots or shoes.

4. At the front of the scene, add more detail to the figures, using pen and bits of paper. You could add faces, hats, bags and gloves.

Glittery garlands

The lines on the crêpe paper should run down, not along, the strip.

1. Unroll a piece of crêpe paper, then cut off a strip about 5cm (2in.) wide. Make it as long as you want your garland to be.

2. Lay the strip of paper on some newspaper and tape down each end. Then, brush a line of glue along the middle of it.

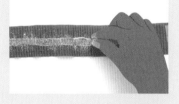

3. Sprinkle the glue with glitter. Leave it to dry, then turn the strip over and decorate it with glitter in the same way.

4. When the glue is almost dry, gently wrap the garland around and around your hand, then carefully slide it off.

The glue dries completely, leaving the garland twisted.

5. Keeping the garland folded, snip along both edges, as far as the glitter stripe. Be careful not to cut all the way through.

6. Unfold the garland, then twist it. Tape it to a work surface and leave it for about three hours before hanging it.

Fairy tree decorations

Use a silver pen
if you have one.

1. Draw around a mug on some paper. Cut out the circle, then fold it in half. Then, unfold the circle and cut along the fold.

2. Draw two arms on one of the half-circles and cut them out. Decorate them with a pen. Then, cut out hands and glue them on.

3. For the body, decorate the second half-circle. Then, to make it into a cone, glue halfway along its straight edge.

Hole

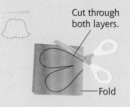

Cut through both layers.

Fold

4. Bend the paper around and press the straight edges together until they stick. Then, cut off the top of the cone, to make a tiny hole.

5. Fold two pieces of paper in half. Draw hair on one and draw a wing on the other, touching the fold. Then, cut out the shapes.

6. Draw a face and cut it out. Glue it onto one of the hair shapes. Then, cut a long piece of thread and fold it in half.

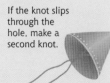

If the knot slips through the hole, make a second knot.

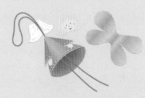

7. Halfway down the piece of thread, tie a knot, to make a loop. Then, push the loop through the hole in the top of the body.

8. Glue the arms onto the body. Glue the loop onto the back part of the hair, then glue the face on top. Glue on the wings.

9. For shoes, thread small beads onto the two pieces of thread hanging down. Then, tie knots below the beads to secure them.

Spots and stars card

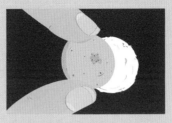

1. Cut two small potatoes in half. Then, use an old spoon to spread a patch of white paint onto a pile of kitchen paper towels.

2. Dip the cut side of a potato into the paint. Print it onto a large piece of red paper. Do this lots of times, until the paper is full of white spots.

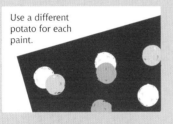

Use a different potato for each paint.

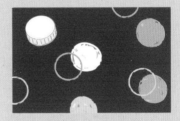

3. Spread some silver and blue paint onto the paper towels and print lots more spots. Make some of them overlap the white ones.

4. For the circles, dip the edge of a bottle top into one of the paints and print it, overlapping some of the spots.

5. For the stars, dip the edge of a piece of cardboard into some paint and print a line. Print two more lines in an 'X' on top.

6. Leave the paint to dry, then cut the paper into several rectangles. Fold each rectangle in half to make a card.

Reindeer collage

1. Cut out several pieces of white paper. Then, rub all over them with pink, orange, white and yellow oil pastels.

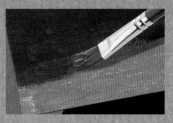

2. Use a thick paintbrush to paint over the pastels with shades of brown or black paint. Let the paint dry.

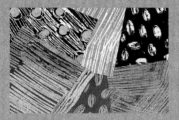

3. Ask an adult to scratch lines and spots in the paint with a craft knife. Vary the width and direction of the lines.

4. Cut simple shapes for a road and houses from the painted papers. Glue them onto a large piece of paper.

5. Cut out simple shapes for a sleigh and glue them onto the paper. Glue presents in and around the sleigh, too.

6. Cut out shapes for the reindeer's head, body, neck, legs, tail and antlers. Glue them on, then add his reins.

Advent castle

1. Rip some white paper to make a snowy hill. Glue it to the bottom of a piece of blue paper.

2. Cut six towers from bright paper, as shown here. Cut a large purple rectangle, too.

3. Lay the rectangle on the hill to show the width of the castle. Glue on the three tallest towers.

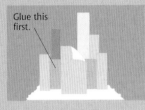

Glue this first.

4. Glue the rectangle over the bottom of the towers. Then, glue the other three towers on top.

5. Cut out six triangles for roofs. Then, glue one roof onto the top of each tower.

6. Cut out 24 doors in different shapes, such as windows, doors, flags and circles.

Draw flagpoles with a silver pen.

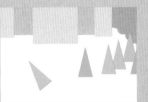

7. Glue one side of each door to the paper. Then, add a little picture under each one.

8. For the trees, cut lots of green paper triangles. Glue them on, overlapping some of them.

9. Fingerprint white spots in the sky for snow. Let them dry. Write numbers 1-24 on the doors.

Pipe cleaner trees

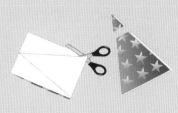

1. Cut a piece of giftwrap that is a little taller than a pipe cleaner. Fold it in half, then bend the end of the pipe cleaner to make a loop.

2. Cut two tall triangles for the tree from the giftwrap. Then, cut across the top of the trees to make two small triangles.

3. Spread glue on one of the triangles, then lay the pipe cleaner on top. Spread glue on the other one and press it on, lining up the edges.

4. Hold the trees together and cut across the top of them again to make two strips. Then, glue the strips onto the pipe cleaner.

5. Continue cutting strips across the trees and gluing them on until they are almost at the bottom of the pipe cleaner.

6. Cut a pot from a folded piece of giftwrap, then glue on the pieces. Press two star stickers onto the pipe cleaner at the top of the tree.

Holly fairy collage

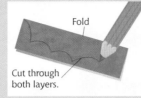
Fold

Cut through
both layers.

Join the points
in the middle.

1. For the fairy's skirt, rip a shape from pink paper. Don't worry if it's uneven. Glue it onto a piece of paper for the background.

2. For the wings, cut green pictures out of a magazine. Fold them in half and draw half a holly leaf on the fold. Then, cut out the leaves.

3. Unfold the leaves and flatten them. Then, glue them onto the background, just above the top of the fairy's skirt.

Use paper from a magazine.

4. Rip a shape that is a little bigger than the skirt, from white tissue paper. Then, gather the tissue paper at the top, like this.

5. Glue the gathered part of the white tissue paper onto the skirt. Then, cut out a body from white paper and glue it on top.

6. Cut out a head, a neck and some hair. Glue the head and neck onto the hair, then draw a face. Glue the head onto the body.

Glue the feet onto some shoes.

Decorate the dress, too.

7. Cut out arms and rip sleeves from paper. Glue them all onto the fairy. Then, cut out feet and glue them on, too.

8. Cut a crown and a strip of paper for a wand and glue them onto the fairy. Add a star sequin or sticker to the end of the wand.

Paper garland

1. Using a pencil, draw a small heart and a slightly larger one on two different shades of pink paper. Then, cut them out.

2. Glue the smaller heart onto the bigger one. Then, using glitter glue, draw around the edge of the smaller heart.

Add spots of glitter glue.

3. Then, brush white glue all over a small piece of bright pink paper. Sprinkle glitter over the top and leave the glue to dry completely.

4. Draw a bell on the back of the paper and cut it out. Cut a paper shape for the top of the bell, then glue it onto the front. Decorate the bell.

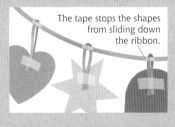

The tape stops the shapes from sliding down the ribbon.

5. Make more shapes. Then, cut pieces of ribbon and fold them in half to make loops. Tape a loop to the back of each shape.

6. Thread the shapes onto a long piece of ribbon and space them out. Then, tape them to the long ribbon with narrow pieces of tape.

113

Sparkling decorations

1. Cut a piece of thread that is about the length of a pencil. Then, cut four strips of kitchen foil about the same length.

2. Fold the thread in half and lay the ends on one of the strips of foil. Scrunch the foil into a ball around the ends and squeeze hard.

Roll the ball on a flat surface.

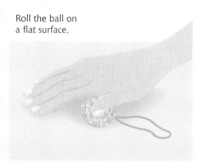

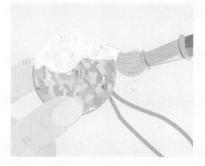

3. Squeeze the other strips of foil around the first one, to make a ball. Then, roll the ball under your hand, to make it round.

4. Brush half of the ball with household glue and sprinkle glitter over it. Leave it to dry, then cover the other half with glitter.

Starry sky

1. Mix lots of watery blue paint and brush it across a large piece of white paper. Make it darker at the bottom of the paper than at the top.

2. When the paint is dry, draw a faint line across the bottom of the paper, for a hill. Then, draw trees and buildings along it.

3. Draw an outline of a Santa and sleigh a little way above the buildings. Add a line of reindeer in front of the sleigh, too.

4. Use black paint or ink to fill in the hill, buildings and trees, so that they make a solid black shape. Leave the paint or ink to dry.

5. Then, fill in the Santa, reindeer and sleigh with a black felt-tip pen. Add a trail of tiny stars behind the sleigh with a silver pen.

6. Draw a moon and lots more stars in the sky with the silver pen. Then, draw rectangles on the buildings for windows.

Glittery fairy bookmark

Use household glue.

1. Cut a circle from paper for the fairy's head. Then, draw a shape for the hair on thick pink paper and cut it out.

2. Cover the hair with glue and sprinkle it with glitter. While the glue dries, cut a strip from the pink paper and glue the head onto it.

Use shiny paper if you have some.

Fold

3. Glue the hair onto the head and draw a face. Then, cut a crown from shiny paper and glue it onto the hair.

4. For wings, fold a piece of thick paper in half and draw a wing on it, like this. Then, keeping the paper folded, cut out the shape.

5. Glue the wings onto the back of the pink strip of paper. Then, decorate the bookmark with stickers, glitter glue and silver pens.

119

Icy snowman

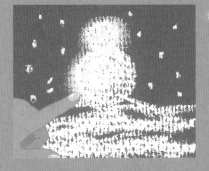

1. Draw a circle with white chalk on blue paper for the head and fill it in. Draw a larger circle below it. Add a wavy line and fill in below it.

2. Draw chalk dots around the snowman. Rub the edge of the snowman with your fingertip to smudge the chalk. Smudge the dots, too.

3. Lay some scrap paper over the bottom of the picture so you don't smudge it any more. Draw black pencil dots for eyes, a mouth and buttons.

4. Draw a nose shaped like a carrot and a scarf around the neck with a bright red pencil. Then, fill them in with red and orange stripes.

Dangly reindeer

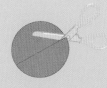

Keep the other piece for later.

1. Lay a small plate on a piece of thick brown paper or thin cardboard. Then, draw around it.

2. Cut out the circle. Fold it in half, then open it out again. Then, cut along the fold, like this.

3. To make a cone, spread glue halfway along the straight edge of one of the half circles.

4. Bend the paper around to make a cone. Then, press and hold the edges together firmly.

5. Cut the tip off the cone. Tie a loop in the middle of a piece of string. Push it through the cone.

6. Draw a reindeer head on the other half circle. Add wavy antlers, ears and a face.

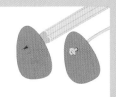

7. Cut out the reindeer's head. Dab glue on the back and press it onto the body.

8. Fold a piece of paper in half. Draw a foot shape on it. Then, cut it out to make two feet.

9. Make a hole in each foot with a pencil. Push the ends of the string through them and knot the ends.

Santa card

1. Fold a square of thick paper in half to make a card. Cut a curved hat from red paper and glue it near the top.

2. Cut a beard with a wavy outline from white paper. Glue it on the card below the hat, leaving a gap between the two.

3. Cut a wavy strip from white paper and glue it on the hat. Press on a white sticker too, or cut one from paper.

4. Cut out a nose from red paper and glue it on. Glue on two circles for eyes, or use stickers. Then, add a smile with a red felt-tip pen.

Holly wrapping paper

1. For the stencil, draw a holly leaf shape on some thick paper. Ask an adult to cut out the shape with a craft knife.

2. Pour some red acrylic paint onto an old plate and spread it out. Dip a piece of kitchen sponge cloth into it.

3. Lay the stencil on a piece of brown wrapping paper. Dab the paint over the stencil, again and again, to print a leaf.

4. Lift the stencil off, then lay it on the paper again, next to the first leaf. Dab paint over the stencil to print another leaf.

5. Stencil three more red leaves in a circle, then stencil green leaves in between the red ones. Leave the paint to dry.

6. Draw a curved line along each green leaf with a gold felt-tip pen. Add a gold spiral in the middle of the leaves.

3-D Christmas trees

You could attach a sparkly
star to the top of the tree.

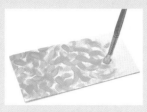  

Scrunch up the tissue paper.

1. Dip a dry paintbrush into green paint, then brush it randomly over a narrow rectangle of paper or cardboard. Let it dry.

2. Then, brush the paper with darker green paint. Before it dries, rub a piece of tissue paper over it to create more texture.

3. When the paint is dry, turn the paper over. Paint blobs of very bright paint all over it. Add some gold blobs too.

  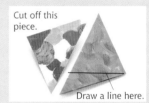

Crease here.

Cut off this piece.

Draw a line here.

4. To make a tree, fold the top right-hand corner of the paper down to the bottom edge. Crease the fold well.

5. Then, hold the right-hand corner and fold it over so that it meets the bottom edge. Crease the fold well.

6. Cut the paper along the edge of the triangle. Then, turn the paper like this, and draw a horizontal line across it.

7. Cut along the line you drew. Unfold the paper, then draw triangles, diamonds and circles all over, avoiding the folds.

8. Ask an adult to cut around each shape with a craft knife, leaving a small part uncut. The uncut part acts like a hinge.

9. Turn the shape over and push up through all the cut shapes. Fold the cardboard into a tree shape and secure it with tape.

Paper angels

1. Draw a curved triangle on thick paper for the angel's dress. Cut it out, then draw and cut out two arms from the same paper.

2. Cut out two hands and glue them onto the arms. Glue one arm behind the dress and one on top of the dress. Then, add two feet.

Hold the layers together.

3. Cut a round head and some hair from paper. Glue the hair onto the head. Then, glue the head onto the top of the dress.

4. To make a zigzag for the wing, fold a rectangle of paper one way, then the other, lots of times. Then, cut off one end at an angle.

5. Cut a piece of thread and tie a big knot in one end. Lay the thread in the middle of the wing, then tape around the end, like this.

6. Tape the wing to the back of the dress. Then, draw a face on the angel and decorate her dress with paper shapes and stickers.

Glittery star chains

Cut the paper at an angle, like this.

The dot shows you which point you folded first.

1. To make a star, put a mug on a piece of paper and draw around it with a pencil. Then, cut out the circle you have drawn.

2. Fold the circle in half, then fold it in half three more times. Then, cut across the folded piece of paper, to make a point.

3. Unfold the star. Draw a pencil dot on one of the points. Then, fold the star in half from this point to the point opposite it.

Press lightly, or you will squash the star.

4. Crease the fold, then open out the star. Fold the next point over to the point opposite it. Then, fold the others in the same way.

5. To make a dip between two points, push the points together. Squash down the fold between them. Repeat this all the way around.

6. Unfold the star and gently press down on its middle, to open out the points a little. Then, make more stars for the chain.

Use a long piece of thread.

7. Brush household glue (PVA) all over the top of a star. Sprinkle glitter over it, then leave it to dry. Then, decorate the other stars.

8. Turn a star over, and put a drop of glue on two opposite points. Then, lay a piece of thread on top of the drops of wet glue.

9. Glue more stars onto the thread and leave the glue to dry. Then, cut off the bottom end of the thread and hang up the chain.

133

Striped camels and kings

1. Paint lines with watery orange and green paint across a piece of thin cardboard. Do them different distances apart.

2. Paint lots more lines across the paper using different paints. Make some of the lines thicker than others.

3. Add some more lines with a thick gold pen or gold paint. Then, turn the cardboard over and paint it with gold paint.

4. When the paint is dry, fold the cardboard in half with the gold paint on the inside. Crease the fold really well.

You could glue on sequins for eyes.

5. Draw a simple outline of a camel on the cardboard. Make sure that its ear and the top of its hump touch the fold.

6. Keeping the cardboard folded, cut around the camel, but don't cut along the fold at the ear or the hump. Then, add eyes.

Frosty branches

Bend and twist
the branch, too.

1. Tear a wide strip of kitchen foil from a roll, then rip it in half. Scrunch one of the pieces of foil as tightly as you can.

2. Scrunch the other piece of foil tightly, too. Then, bend and twist both pieces to make wiggly twig shapes.

3. Tear another wider strip of foil and rip it in half. Scrunch it tightly around the ends of the two twigs to hold them together.

You'll get two identical leaves.

4. Repeat steps 1-3 to make another branch. Then, join the two branches together with another piece of foil.

5. Fold a piece of tracing paper or tissue paper in half. Draw a simple leaf shape. Then, cut it out, keeping the paper folded.

6. Spread glue on one leaf and press the end of a twig onto it. Lay the other leaf on top, sandwiching the twig between them.

7. Cut out more pairs of leaves and glue them around the ends of all the twigs in the same way. Then, let the glue dry.

8. Brush both sides of the leaves with household glue. Sprinkle the glue with glitter, then shake off any excess, when it is dry.

Shiny ornament card

Use shiny paper if you have it.

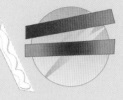

1. For a long card, fold a rectangle of thick paper in half, with its long sides together, and crease the fold well.

2. Draw around several small jar lids on the back of pieces of wrapping paper. Cut out the circles you have drawn.

3. For a striped ornament, cut strips of shiny paper. Glue them across one of the circles, letting the strips overlap the edges.

4. When the glue is dry, turn the ornament over. Then, cut off the ends of the strips that overlap the edge of the circle.

5. To make an ornament with stars, press star stickers onto one of your shiny circles. Make some of them overlap the edges.

6. Trim off all the extra pieces of the stickers that are overlapping the edges of the circle, as you did before.

7. Decorate the other shiny circles with different patterns of stripes, stars and circles. Use stickers or cut shapes from paper.

8. Glue the circles onto the card at different levels. Use a felt-tip pen to draw a string from the top of the card to each ornament.

139

Foil bird decorations

 Use a glue stick.

1. Cut a large piece of foil from a roll of kitchen foil. Spread glue all over the non-shiny side, then fold the foil in half, like this.

2. Lay the folded foil on top of an old magazine. Then, gently rub the foil so that the layers stick together and the surface is smooth.

3. Using a ballpoint pen, draw the outline of a bird's body and beak on the foil. Add wings, an eye and two legs. Press hard as you draw.

4. Add some lines for the tail, making them end with a curl. Add more curved lines on the head and wings, and spirals on the tummy.

5. Use scissors to cut around the bird, a little way from the outlines. Tape a loop of thread to the back for hanging. Then, make more birds.

Reindeer decorations

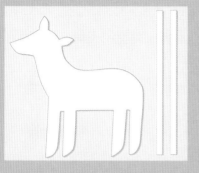

1. Draw the outline of a reindeer on a piece of thin cardboard and cut it out. Then, cut two long, thin strips from cardboard. These are for the antlers.

2. Paint the reindeer with thick, red paint. Quickly, before the paint dries, use a toothpick to scratch patterns in the paint. Paint the strips and scratch a line along them.

Tape the antlers on the back of the head.

3. Cut one of the strips in half, then cut the remaining strip into smaller pieces. Glue the short pieces onto the longer ones to make two antlers. Tape them onto the head.

Snow fairy card

1. Fold a piece of blue paper in half. Then, lay a mug on white paper. Draw around it and cut out the circle.

2. Mix some paint for the fairy's face and body. Paint a face on the circle. Then, paint a body below it.

3. Paint four shapes for the fairy's wings. Paint her hair and a small yellow circle for the end of the wand.

4. When the paint is dry, outline the fairy's dress, chin and wings with a thin black pen. Decorate her dress, too.

5. Draw a face, then add arms, feet and lines on the fairy's hair. Draw a wand with a star on the end.

6. Glue the circle onto the card. Paint a white line from the top of the card and add a bow and spots.

145

Pretty snowflakes

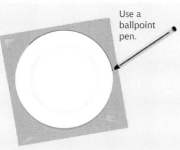

Use a ballpoint pen.

1. Cut a piece of cellophane from some packaging. Put a saucer on top and draw around it. Cut out the circle.

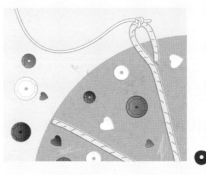

Curl this end around for hanging.

2. Cut a piece of string wider than the circle. Paint it with household glue and press it on the cellophane, like this.

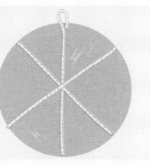

3. Cut two more pieces of string about the width of the circle. Paint them with glue. Lay them over the first one in an 'X' shape.

4. When the glue is dry, decorate the snowflake by gluing on sequins or adding stickers. Tie some thread around the loop for hanging.

Trees in winter

Draw the tree trunks bending at different angles.

Make the zigzags a triangular shape.

1. Draw a tree trunk with a blue felt-tip pen on a piece of paper. Then, add branches coming from the trunk. Add little twigs on the branches.

2. Draw lots more trees in the same way. Draw large ones at the bottom of the paper and much smaller ones at the top.

3. Draw green zigzag trees in between the other trees. Draw a short line for a trunk at the bottom. Fill in any spaces with purple trees.

4. Add dots for snow across the paper with a white wax crayon – they are shown here in yellow so that you can see them.

5. Draw some hills above the trees with a pencil. Then, mix some watery blue paint. Fill in the hills and paint a shadow beneath each tree.

6. When the hills are dry, mix some darker blue paint and brush it across the sky. Then, leave the painting to dry completely.

7. Dip a clean paintbrush into some water, then brush it around and around on top of one of the trees. The ink will run in the water.

8. Brush water over all the other blue trees. Then, brush water over the green and purple trees, rinsing your brush each time.

Bead decorations

1. Cut a piece of giftwrap that is as long as a fat straw. Make it the same height as your little finger.

2. Spread glue over the back of the giftwrap. Lay the straw along one edge and roll it tightly in the paper.

3. Cover more straws with different kinds of giftwrap. For a very long chain you will need to cover five straws.

4. When the glue is dry, cut the straws into different sizes of beads. Cut some long and some short ones.

5. Thread a blunt needle with strong thread. Tape the long end of the thread to a work surface.

6. Thread on all the beads. Then, push the needle back through the last bead and knot the ends of the thread.

Painted angels

1. Mix some watery blue paint. Then, paint curved shapes for the angels' dresses on a piece of thick white paper.

2. While the paint is still wet, mix some slightly thicker blue paint. Paint lines, dots or patterns on the dresses.

3. Mix some paint for the angels' skin. Use it to paint a round face and lines for arms and legs on each angel, like this.

4. Using thick gold paint, paint two wings above the arms. Then, add a circle for the halo, leaving a gap above the face.

5. Use a thin paintbrush to add the hair. Paint a different hairstyle on each angel. Then, add red circles for rosy cheeks.

6. When the paint is dry, outline the angels with a black pen. Draw their faces and add details, such as bows and shoes.

153

Coconut mice

To make about eight large mice, five medium mice
and three baby mice, you will need:

- 250g / 9oz / 2 cups icing sugar*, sifted
- 200g / 8oz / 1 cup of condensed milk
- 175g / 7oz / 3 cups of shredded or
  desiccated coconut
- red food dye
- white chocolate for ears
- edible cake-decorating balls

*In the US, use powdered sugar.

1. Mix the icing sugar and the condensed milk together in a bowl. Mix in the coconut. Put the mixture into two bowls.

2. Add a few drops of red dye to each bowl and mix it in. Then add a few more drops of dye to one of the bowls.

3. Dip a clean tablespoon into some water and let it drip. Then, lift out a big spoonful of the mixture.

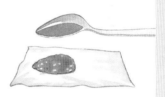

4. Pat the spoonful smooth on top. Turn the spoon over and put the shape onto a piece of plastic foodwrap.

5. Pinch a nose at the thinner end of the spoon shape. Add white chocolate for ears and cake-decorating balls for eyes.

6. Push a piece of liquorice under the shape, as a tail. Leave the mouse to harden on a plate. Make more mice.

Jolly Santas

1. Use a pencil to draw a circle for a head and another one for the body. Then, draw curved lines for the arms and legs.

2. Dip your finger into some thick red paint, then finger paint a hat on top of the head. Finger paint the body, arms and legs, too.

Overlap the prints for the boots.

3. Finger paint brown blobs on the end of each arm, for mittens. Then, do two overlapping fingerprints for each boot.

4. Mix some paint for the face, then finger paint the face and ears. When the paint is dry, print a darker nose and slightly paler cheeks.

5. Unravel a cotton ball. Pull off little pieces for the cuffs, and pieces for the hat and the bottom of the jacket. Then, glue them all on.

6. Tear a long beard from the cotton ball and two smaller pieces for whiskers. Glue them on, then draw the eyes with a black felt-tip pen.

Glittering shapes

1. Place a big cookie cutter on a slice of white bread. Press it firmly, to cut out the shape.

2. Very carefully, push the bread shape out of the cutter, so that the bread doesn't tear.

3. Press the end of a drinking straw through one of the points of the star, to make a hole.

4. Put the bread shape onto a wire rack and leave it overnight to become hard.

5. Mix a little paint with white glue. Then, paint it on the edges of the star shape.

6. Paint the top of the bread shape. When it is dry, turn it over and paint the other side.

7. Glue lots of glitter onto the top of the shape. Add sequins and tiny beads, too.

8. Push a long piece of thread through the hole, then make a loop at the end of the thread.

9. Push the ends of the thread through the loop. Then, tie a knot and pull it tight.

159

Ice fairies

1. Pour some white paint onto an old plate. Then, cut a rectangle from thick cardboard and dip one edge into the paint.

2. To make a skirt, place the edge of the cardboard on some paper. Scrape it around, keeping the top end in the same place.

3. To make the body, dip the edge of a shorter piece of cardboard into the paint. Then, place it above the skirt and drag it across.

4. Mix some paint for the skin. Dip the end of another piece of cardboard into the paint. Press it onto the paper, to print arms.

5. Cut a small cardboard rectangle and print a neck and two feet. Then, dip your fingertip into the paint and print a head.

6. When the head is dry, spread a little blue paint onto the plate. Then, dip your finger into the paint and fingerprint some hair.

The part you're holding will stay sticky.

7. For the wings, sprinkle a little glitter onto some newspaper. Hold a piece of sticky tape at one end and dip it into the glitter.

8. Dip a second piece of tape into the glitter. Then, cut a corner off each piece of tape, away from the sticky end, like this.

9. Press the sticky ends of the wings onto the fairy. Then, fold them back and press them down, so that the glitter is on the front.

Snowman chain

1. Lay two pieces of thin paper side by side, with their short edges together. Then, join them with tape.

2. Fold the paper in half along the join. Then, fold each half to make a zigzag, like this.

3. Draw a snowman's hat at the top of the paper. Draw a head below it, and a band all the way across for his arms.

4. Add a big round tummy below the arms. Draw some fat legs, then add feet at the end of the legs.

5. Outline the snowman with a black felt-tip pen. Cut along the outline, but don't cut along the folds at the arms.

6. Open out the chain. Then, fill in the hats and add faces and buttons. Decorate each snowman in a different way.

Paper snowflakes

1. Put a mug on top of a piece of white paper. Then draw lightly around the mug with a pencil.

2. Using a pair of scissors, cut out the circle you have drawn. Fold the circle in half, then fold it in half again.

3. Cut triangles of different sizes from each edge of the folded shape. Cut off the pointed tip, too.

4. Open out the circle. The cut-out pattern makes a snowflake. Glue sequins and glitter onto it.

5. Place the mug on a piece of tissue paper. Draw around it, then cut out the circle of tissue paper.

6. Dab spots of white glue onto the back of the snowflake. Then, press on the tissue paper circle.

Penguin picture

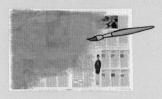

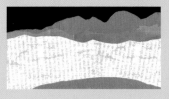

1. Use a thick brush to paint some pieces of old newspaper with blue and white paint. Leave them to dry.

2. Cut out shapes for the sea, ice and mountains. Glue them onto a large piece of black paper.

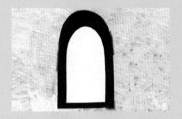

3. To make a penguin, cut out a shape for a body from paper. Cut out another shape for its head and tummy.

4. Glue them onto the background, then use black pen to draw a beak, eyes and two flippers.

5. For a baby penguin, cut out a body from paper. Cut a head shape out of paper, and then another shape to glue on top.

6. Glue the head onto the body, then glue the penguin onto the bckground. Draw on an eye, a beak and a flipper.

Christmas tree star

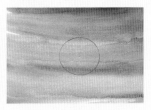

1. Brush shades of purple paint across a piece of thick paper. When it's dry, paint the other side of the paper, too.

2. Brush glue on one side, then sprinkle a little glitter all over it. When the glue is dry, do the same to the other side.

3. Place a saucer that measures around 15cm (6in.) across, on the paper. Draw around it, then draw a dot in the middle.

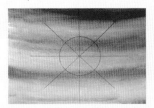

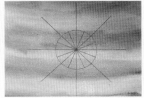

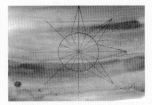

4. Draw four long lines through the middle. Make them come out about the same distance outside the circle.

5. Draw short lines in between each of the long lines, starting at the middle and stopping at the edge of the circle.

6. Draw the points of the star, by connecting the end of each short line to the end of a long line. Then, cut out the star.

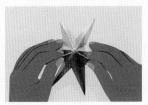

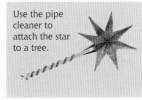

Use the pipe cleaner to attach the star to a tree.

7. Ask an adult to score along the straight lines using a craft knife, without cutting all the way through.

8. To make the star 3-D, pinch the long lines upwards and fold the short lines downwards. Crease the folds well.

9. Glue a pipe cleaner on one of the points. Twist the pipe cleaner around a pencil, then stretch it a little to open it up.

Marzipan snowmen

Mix it in with your fingers.

1. Break a large piece of white marzipan into quarters. Then, put each quarter into a small bowl.

2. Add several drops of red food dye to one of the quarters. Mix it in until the marzipan is red.

3. Mix green dye into one quarter and yellow into another. Don't mix dye into the last quarter.

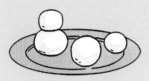

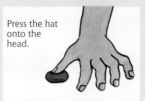

Press the hat onto the head.

Add dots for a face using a toothpick.

4. Roll some of the plain marzipan into a ball. Roll a smaller ball for the head and press it on top.

5. Roll a ball of red marzipan for a hat. Press it flat and add a tiny red ball on top.

6. Roll a sausage from red marzipan and wrap it around the snowman's neck for a scarf.

7. For a present, roll a ball of red marzipan. Press the flat side of a knife down on the ball.

8. Turn the ball on its side and press it with the knife again. Do this until the ball becomes a cube.

9. Roll sausages of green marzipan and press them onto the cube, like this. Add loops for a bow.

* Don't give marzipan to people who are allergic to nuts.

Sparkly garland

1. For a round ornament, draw around a mug on a piece of bright paper. Draw a small shape at the top for hanging.

2. Cut out the ornament. Then, cut a strip of paper and glue it across the middle. Press on stickers or glue on paper stars.

3. For the hanger, draw a rectangle with a circle on top, on shiny paper. Cut it out, then cut a zigzag along the bottom.

4. Fold the paper and snip a piece out of the middle of the circle to make a hole. Glue the hanger on the top of the ornament.

5. Draw a long, thin ornament. Cut three curved strips and glue them on. Make a hanger for the top and glue it on.

6. Spread stripes of glue across the ornament, then sprinkle it with glitter. Shake off any extra glitter when the glue is dry.

The tape stops the shapes from slipping.

7. Use a hole punch to make a hole at the top of a tree, cut from green paper. Cut a rectangle of paper and glue it on the bottom.

8. Decorate the tree with paper shapes, stickers and sequins. You could also add dots of glitter or glitter glue.

9. Push a piece of ribbon, thread or string through each ornament. Secure them to the ribbon with a thin piece of tape.

Ice queen

Draw curls on the end of the sleeves.

1. Draw a heart-shaped head, then add a face and ears. Draw a crown above the face and add wavy lines around it for the hair.

2. Draw a neck and add a curved collar. Draw the arms and add hands with pointed fingers. Add sleeves, and a cloak billowing behind her.

The lines are shown here in yellow so that you can see them.

3. Draw a long body and a flowing skirt with swirling curls at the bottom. Then, go over all the pencil lines with a blue pencil.

4. Draw more curls on the dress with a white wax crayon. Draw lines in the hair and cloak, and add some coming from the fingers.

5. Paint clean water all over the paper to make it damp. Then, blob turquoise ink or watery paint onto the paper around the queen.

6. Then, brush very watery paint or ink onto the body while the paper is still damp. Paint darker dots and swirls too. Then, let the paint dry.

Spangly star wand

1. Draw a star on a piece of cardboard and cut it out. Then, put the star onto the cardboard again and draw around it.

Keep the marks at the top of the stars.

2. Draw a mark at the top of the first star, then move it off the cardboard. Draw a mark at the top of the second star, then cut it out.

The slots need to be the same length.

3. Keeping the marks at the top, cut a slot in each star, like this. Make the slots the same thickness as the cardboard.

4. Cut a rectangle from a roll of kitchen foil, making it a little longer and several times wider than a drinking straw.

5. Lay the foil on some old newspaper and cover the non-shiny side with glue. Then, lay the straw on top, near one edge of the foil.

Squash the end of the straw.

6. Roll the straw, so that the foil sticks all the way around it. Then, tape the straw onto the star with a slot at the top.

Hold the straw in place.

7. Hold the star with the slot at the bottom, above the star with the slot at the top. Then, push the stars together, like this.

Use household glue.

8. Rip up lots of strips of tissue paper and glue them all over the stars. Cover the stars with two or three layers of tissue paper.

9. Brush the stars with glue and sprinkle them with glitter. Glue on beads and sequins, or shapes cut from shiny paper.

Night animals

Drag the paint to make thicker lines.

1. Dip the edge of a piece of cardboard into thick white paint, then print a trunk and branches on a piece of blue paper.

2. Fingerprint an owl's body, and use the end of a paintbrush to print the eyes. Then, draw a beak and add patterns for feathers.

3. For a bat, fingerprint a body. Then, paint the wings and let them dry. Draw lines on the wings with chalk.

4. Print yellow eyes with the end of a paintbrush. Draw dots in the eyes, then add feet and ears.

Twist the cardboard to print a triangle.

Draw around the tail, too.

5. For a fox, dip the edge of a piece of cardboard into orange paint. Then, print a triangular head.

6. Fingerpaint a body and tail. Then, print the legs with cardboard. Draw ears, eyes and a nose when the paint is dry.

179

Snowy skaters

Add the ear halfway down.

1. Rip different pictures of clothes from old magazines. Use a pencil to draw a sweater and a hat on the pictures, then cut them out.

2. Glue the sweater onto a large piece of white paper. Draw an oval head above it with a blue felt-tip pen, then add the eyes.

3. Draw a mouth and some hair and fill them in. Draw mittens at the end of each sleeve with a paler pen. Then, draw a skirt and fill it in, too.

4. Draw two curved legs and add feet. Fill in the legs and feet. Then, draw two short lines and a curved blade for each ice skate.

5. Glue the hat on the top of the head. Then, draw several more skaters in the same way, using ideas from the picture to the left.

6. Draw a little fence around the skaters for the edge of the pond. Draw curved lines for tracks on the ice. Then, add trees behind the pond.

Cut-paper tree

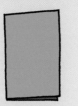

1. Cut a square of bright green paper or thin cardboard. Then, fold it in half and crease it well.

2. Using a pencil and a ruler, draw a line on the paper, from the top of the fold to the opposite corner.

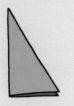

3. Keeping the paper folded, cut along the pencil line to make a tall triangle. Don't unfold the paper yet.

4. Cut a triangle near the top of the folded edge. Then, cut another one from the other side.

5. Cut another triangle from the fold, then one on the other side. Then, cut more triangles from both sides.

6. Carefully open out the tree shape and flatten it. Then, decorate it with shiny paper shapes or stickers.

Star card

Shake off the extra glitter when the glue is dry.

1. Draw three stars on a piece of bright paper and cut them out.

2. Put a blob of glue on each star and sprinkle it with glitter.

Glue under here.

3. Cut three strips of thin paper. Glue a strip to the back of each star.

4. Fold a piece of thick paper in half. Glue the stars onto it, like this.

5. When the glue is dry, stand the card up. The stars will fall forward.

185

Snowflake patterns

1. Use a pale blue pencil to draw four lines that cross each other in the middle. Then, draw four more lines with a blue ballpoint pen.

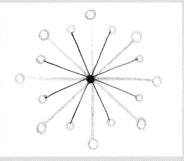

2. Draw a circle in the middle with the pen and fill it in. Then, add a circle to the end of each line with the blue pencil.

3. Draw small leaf-shaped patterns along all of the pencil lines. You'll find it easier if you turn your paper as you draw them.

Tiny Christmas cookies

To make about 65 tiny cookies, you will need:

* 50g / 2oz / 4 tablespoons butter, softened
* 25g / 1oz / ¼ cup icing sugar*
* 8 drops of red food dye
* 1 teaspoon of milk
* ¼ teaspoon of vanilla extract
* 75g / 3oz / ¾ cup plain/ all-purpose flour
* little star and heart cutters

Before you start, wipe two baking sheets with cooking oil.
Heat your oven to 180°C, 350°F, gas mark 4.

*In the US, use powdered sugar.

1. Put the butter into a bowl and stir it until it is creamy. Sift the sugar into the bowl and stir it in until the mixture is smooth.

2. Add the food dye to the mixture and stir it in until the mixture is pink. Then, add the milk and the vanilla extract.

3. Sift the flour into the bowl and stir everything together. Then, use your hands to squeeze the mixture into a dough.

Cut the shapes close together.

4. Dust a rolling pin and a clean work surface with flour. Roll out the dough until it is slightly thinner than your little finger.

5. Use the cutters to cut lots of shapes from the dough. Then, use a spatula to lift the shapes onto the baking sheets.

6. Squeeze the scraps of dough together to make a ball. Roll out the dough again and cut more shapes. Put them onto the sheets.

Wear oven mitts.

7. Make patterns on some of the cookies by pushing the end of a toothpick into them. Don't worry if it goes all the way through.

8. Bake the cookies for six to eight minutes. Then, take them out of the oven and leave them on the trays until they are cool.

Handprinted angel

This is the angel's dress upside-down.

1. For the dress, press your hand in blue paint, then press it in the middle of some paper.

2. Press both hands into some yellow paint. Make two prints a little lower, for the wings.

3. Turn your paper. Dip your finger in pink paint, then go around and around, for a head.

4. Use your fingertip to do blue arms. Join them to the dress. Add some hands, too.

5. Use orange paint to finger paint some hair. Then, add a yellow halo above the head.

6. Fingerprint some eyes and a nose. Then, use your little fingertip to paint a smiling mouth.

191

Snowy hill

1. Draw a curve for a hill on a piece of dark blue paper. Fill it in with white paint. Then, draw stars in the sky with a white pencil or chalk.

2. For a house, draw a square with a dark pink felt-tip pen on a piece of pink or purple paper. Add a pointed roof and a chimney.

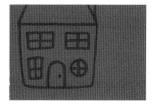

3. Draw some windows and a door on the house. Then, add crossed lines inside each window, and a handle on the door.

4. Draw rows of U-shapes for tiles on the roof. Then, fill in the tiles with a white pencil, making sure you don't go over any felt-tip pen lines.

5. Fill in the wall of the house with a lilac pencil. Make the windows orange and blue, and the door red. Fill in the chimney with lilac.

6. Draw a large triangle for a Christmas tree with a dark pink felt-tip pen. Add a small trunk at the bottom of the tree, like this.

7. Draw three zigzag lines across the tree to look like branches. Then, draw a star at the top of the tree and fill it in with an orange pencil.

8. Fill in the top of the tree with a white pencil, then use different shades of blue and green pencils to fill in lower branches.

9. Draw several more houses and trees in the same way. Then, cut them out. Arrange them on the snowy hill, then glue them on.

193

Printed star wrapping paper

1. You will need a large cookie cutter and a potato that is bigger than the cutter.

2. Carefully cut a slice from the middle of the potato. Press the cookie cutter into the slice.

3. Push out the shape you have cut. You may need some help with the last two steps.

4. Dab both sides of the potato shape on some kitchen paper towels to dry it.

5. Press a fork into the shape. This will stop you from getting too messy when you print.

6. Pour two or three small patches of paint onto an old newspaper. Do them close together.

7. Dip the potato shape into the middle of the paint, then press it onto a piece of paper.

8. Dip the shape into the paint again, then print it. Fill the paper with lots of printed shapes.

You could wrap presents in your printed paper and tie a shiny ribbon around them.

Twinkly Christmas tree

Press hard as
you draw.

The white
crayon lines
are shown
in yellow so
that you can
see them.

1. Draw a line for the floor
across the bottom of a
piece of white paper with
a light green wax crayon.
Draw a tree, its pot and
a star.

2. Draw some presents
beneath the tree. Then,
use a white wax crayon
to draw stars around the
tree and add spots on
it, too.

3. Mix lots of watery
yellow paint, then brush
it all over the paper. The
wax crayon lines and
shapes will resist the
paint. Leave it to dry.

Paint
some
orange
presents,
too.

Use a felt-tip
pen to draw
the strings
and bows.

4. Brush watery pink
paint over the tree,
presents and floor. While
it is still wet, dot yellow
and orange paint on the
tree. Fill in the star, too.

5. When the paint is
dry, draw large round
decorations and
candy canes with
thick white paint or
correction fluid.

6. Draw hearts on the
tree with a red pencil.
Add strings and bows to
some of the decorations.
Draw stripes on the
candy canes, too.

7. Spread white glue on
the big white decorations
and sprinkle them with
glitter. Put dots of glue
on the star and sprinkle it
with glitter, too.

8. Draw around the
glittery decorations with
a bright pink pencil. Add
a shape at the top for
hanging and fill it in with
a paler pink pencil.

9. To make the tree
twinkly, blob little dots
of glue onto the tree,
Then, press a sparkly
sequin or bead onto
each blob of glue.

Painted chalets

Press gently as you draw.

1. On thick paper, draw a ski chalet with some steps. Then, add pointed shapes for hills, and curved lines for mountains.

2. Paint the sky and hills with pale blue watery paints. Let the paint dry, then paint the sky again to make it darker.

3. Paint different parts of the chalet with pale paints. Let each patch of paint dry before painting the next one.

4. Add details, such as shutters and a balcony, with a thin brush. When all the paint has dried, draw details with pencils.

Tree card

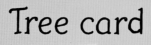

Save this half for later.

1. Cut a big rectangle of thick paper or thin cardboard. Fold it in half, long sides together.

2. Get some help to cut a large potato in half from end to end. Cut one half into a tall triangle.

Spread the paint with the back of a spoon.

Dip the potato into the paint each time you print a shape.

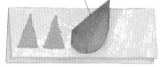

3. Lay some kitchen paper towels onto some old newspapers. Pour green paint on top.

4. Dip the potato into the paint and press it onto your card. Print more trees along the card.

5. Cut a square of potato. Dip it in red paint and print it below each tree.

You could add star stickers to the tops of the trees.

Tree decorations

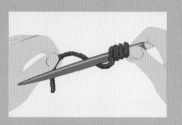

1. Hold one end of a pipe cleaner against the handle of a thin paintbrush. Wind the rest of the pipe cleaner tightly around the handle.

2. When the whole pipe cleaner is wound around the handle, slide it off. Hold both ends and pull them gently to stretch it a little.

3. Make nine more curly pipe cleaners. Then, lay all ten pipe cleaners on a piece of thread. Tie a knot in the middle of the pipe cleaners.

4. Bend all the pipe cleaners in different directions. Then, knot the ends of the thread, to make a loop for hanging the decoration.

5. For an icicle decoration, bend over the tip of a pipe cleaner. Then, wrap the pipe cleaner tightly around itself, to make a flat spiral.

6. To make the icicle, hold the outside of the spiral and pull out the middle. Then, tie a piece of thread around the top end for hanging.

Index

Written by Fiona Watt, Rebecca Gilpin, Anna Milbourne, Leonie Pratt, Ray Gibson and Catherine Atkinson.

Designed & illustrated by Non Figg, Kate Fearn, Antonia Miller, Josephine Thompson, Katie Lovell, Erica Harrison, Jan McCafferty and Amanda Gulliver.